I'D RATHER BE
ON AN ISLAND

JABRI HARRISON

PURPOSE GANG PUBLISHING

I'd Rather Be On An Island

Copyright © 2019 by Jabri Harrison

PURPOSE GANG PUBLISHING

DEDICATION

A couple years ago, I prayed for God to take the people out of my life that weren't benefiting my growth. I asked Him to replace them with great people that would help me become who I'm meant to be. He has answered that prayer 10 fold. God gave me everything I needed to write this book. I didn't do anything except put my name on it. All my accomplishments and things that I've done can be attributed to the people God has sent to my life and to accepting His invitations. If you are connected to me, you are God sent and I thank Him for you. There are too many to name, but I'd like to say thank you. I appreciate you and value you.

TABLE OF CONTENTS

INTRO

Life has been rough, and after a bad day, I come home to a letter in the mail from God. I've heard of His name, but I don't know His face. In the letter, I'm invited on a trip full of love, kindness, joy, goodness, long suffering, faithfulness, gentleness, and freedom. I don't know what long-suffering is so I ignore it, because all the other things sound great. I don't know exactly who this God is so I look Him up, Google Him, and ask everybody I know. I get some bad responses, but mostly good, so I decide to go. Pastor Angela Beard, a great woman of God, once told me, "Seeking for God turns into a process of learning God."

I always said I'd rather be on an island. There would be no people. It would be a place where there is no need for money, which means no waking up early for a job. I would enjoy long sunny days, with a cool breeze, and the warm sand between my toes. I love seafood and fruit as well. There would be no need to cook because fruit would just fall into my mouth as I'm lying on the beach stress-free.

This trip sounds just like that, so I pack my things and go on my way. In life, we have to be careful about what we wish (pray) for because the tongue has the power of life and death.

When I make it to the ship, I meet the beautiful, wonderful, and powerful captain–Jesus. I think it's a little odd that I'm the only one on the ship, but for some reason inside me, I trust the captain and believe that the others are missing out. As I move further away from the shore, I get settled in and comfortable–smooth sailing.

I wake up on an island shipwrecked. I wish it all was a dream, but it's real.

SECTION 1

CHAPTER 1

YOUR INFLUENCE

CALL OUT FOR HELP!

Jeremiah 33:3 (NKJV): "Call to me, and I will answer you, and show you great and mighty things, which you do not know."

In life, we all reach a point in our life where we feel like we have lost everything and we have nothing left. Whether we got ourselves into it or life has just knocked us down. Things happen in life that are outside of our control. There are things that happen to us that are an effect of our personal choices. Those may have an instant effect or may have effects long down the line. We all at some point in life hit a low. We have no strength left and nothing left to give.

From my observation, this is usually a divine opportunity to call out to Jesus. If we get out of this situation, we know that it was God and nothing we did. These divine situations humble us. They force us to make a decision. Do we want to continue to go down this road under our own power or do we want God's will and to let Him take the wheel? To continue to try and have our way or to pick up our cross and die to ourselves? This place is where we look in the mirror and ask ourselves, "Who am I and what is my purpose? My answer is, "No matter where I go, no matter what happens, God, I am yours, and I only want you." What is your answer? Your ship has wrecked on this island, and all that you know is gone. Call out for help! The same word that is used in the Bible for this "call" can be replaced by "cry." Cry unto the Lord!

DON'T WAIT FOR SOMEONE ELSE TO SAVE YOU

Philippians 3:13–14 (NKJV): "Brethren, I do not count myself to have apprehended; but one thing I do, forgetting those things which are behind and reaching forward to those things which are ahead, I press toward the goal for the prize of the upward call of God in Christ Jesus."

Waking up on this island shipwrecked was life-changing. Everything was going so good. This is not the trip I expected. Everything is gone. I have cried out with all my might. I can't muster up the strength to scream any louder. All that I've known can't currently help me. I have to forget what happened in the past. I can't move forward looking back. I have to press on!

The world and the past tell you that your past is who you are. There have been people in your life that have spoken things over you that are lies because God hasn't said those things about you. God says so much more. God, even before He made the earth, loved and chose you. God knitted you in your mother's womb. Before you were born, you were set apart. God made you beautiful, perfectly designed you for a time such as now. You are His masterpiece, created anew in Jesus Christ so that you can complete the good things He planned for you long ago. He has ordered your steps and has plans for good and not for disaster, to give you a future and a hope. Trust in these things and do not trust another man to save the day. Get up, forget the past and press on.

PICK UP THE PIECES

Now what? After I get myself together, I look around, and everything is still broken. Parts of the ship, clothes, luggage, and more are scattered all over the sandy shore. Most of it is wet, but I start looking for the things that are still of use and make a big pile of those things. While I do this, God is showing me that there are some things He wants me to keep and some things He wants me to throw out because where He is taking me, some of the old things will be useless and will only hold me back.

Imagine going up a huge island mountain with everything plus your junk. It will only weigh you down and slow you down. Those things that you lug around that aren't helpful in your life are burdens you can't afford to hold onto. Even some of the old things that meant a lot to you. This doesn't mean that ever old thing is worthless though. God divinely had you pick up things in the past to help you in your future. I'm not talking about that old necklace your ex gave you back in high school but rather the things that people in your life have helped you realize. These things include your gifts, habits you picked up that equip you to become more efficient, and tools that will help you to fix things in the future. These things that you acquired through your life can be very beneficial.

Now that you have cried out to God and given up what your past has said about you, it's time to pick up the pieces.

ORGANIZE YOUR LIFE

Now I have a pile of things I want to keep, but because I tried to keep it light, I had to make some hard decisions. In the pile, I find a briefcase with flash cards, multiple colored pens, a Bible, and notebooks. I also find in the sand a cross with writing on it. It says, "Pick up your cross and die to yourself daily." I put it into my short pockets, and I'm starting to feel like my anxiety, stress, and sadness are leaving. I take one of the notebooks and start journaling in it. (P.S. if there isn't a notebook in your brief case there is one at your local crab shack down the shore.) Most of my journaling is about my desires, wishes, and daily struggles. I take out another notebook and label it "prayers." Then I start skimming through the Bible and write some of my favorite verses on the flash cards. I color coordinate them to help me remember them, and I plan to do this all daily. In another notebook, I write down some goals. The first goal I write down is to find my purpose. I start to organize my life. Then, I look at my first goal again, and I ask myself who am I?

It's hard making decisions on things that matter so much to you. There is gonna be friends that you are going to want to keep, even though you know they are bad for you. They have been around for a long time, you are comfortable with them, they know you, and you trust them. That's the same way you feel about the other things that you need to let go. You have to trust that God has something better for you and that those things you are trying to hold onto won't even compare to what you have ahead of you. You have to make room for new things. Once you have made the hard decisions, organize the things you do have. Get to know those things and where they are at. Find things that can help you keep organized. A planner is a great way to organize your time, know your goals, and decide when you want to complete them.

DON'T LOSE YOURSELF

Hebrews 6:11-12 (ESV): "And we desire that each one of you show the same diligence to the full assurance of hope until the end, that you do not become sluggish, but imitate those who through faith and patience inherit the promises."

It's hot, I haven't eaten, and I've been through a lot in a short amount of time. It seems like the world, my situation, and my mind is beating me right now. I want to give up, but something inside me is telling me not to give up and not to grow lazy. A voice tells me I have great things ahead. The sun is setting, and there is a beautiful sunset. "Who am I in this new place?" I wonder. I'm on an island, but I'm not going to lose myself.

You're not yourself when you're hungry, so it's important that you eat on every word of the Bible. The world, your environment, and your situation will try to tell you who you are, how you should be, and how you should feel. Instead, you need to let your creator tell you who you are, how you should be, and what you should feel. You are a child of God. You're never alone. God is with you. There are many great men and women in the Bible that fulfilled their destiny and purpose through their faith. Spend time learning about them, identify the characteristics that match yours, and learn from the ones you don't have. Imitate their faith, hope, and trust in God.

Who is your favorite person in the Bible and why? Jesus should be one. Think of a couple more and write down their characteristics in your journal.

GET TO KNOW YOURSELF

Today was a good day. I had already organized my life, and I decided that I wasn't gonna lose myself. Everything has settled down, and now I have to get myself together. The question I asked myself the other day was, "Who am I on this island? Really, who am I—period?" Today, I sat down and read through the Bible to find out the answer.

To fulfill your purpose, you have to know who you are. Your whole life, you always felt like you were different. What people saw in you didn't match up with how you felt inside. You didn't fit in with everybody's circles, and you didn't fit in with the squares. You didn't fit into the spaces they try to put you in. It's because you are bigger than that. You are a child of God. You have a great power inside of you.

1 John 4:4 says, "You are of God, little children, and have overcome them because He who is in you is greater than he who is in the world." You have to realize the power you have. You are a kingdom shifter. You have divine weapons. You are the light that casts out darkness. You are made to look different from the world. That's why they don't invite you. They wonder why you don't look and act like them. They don't want you around because you are a mirror. They see their flaws when you are around. They are convicted by their sin. With that being said, however, you can't dim your light to fit in. Read the Bible and believe what God says about you. Soon you will come to the knowledge of who you are and who you are not.

PRAYER

WRITE YOUR OWN HERE

CHAPTER 2

NEW PLACES

SCOPE YOUR SURROUNDINGS

Isaiah 6:8-9 (NKJV): "Also I heard the voice of the Lord, saying: 'Whom shall I send, and who will go for Us?' Then I said, 'Here am I! Send me.' And He said, 'Go, and tell these people: 'Keep on hearing, but do not understand; Keep on seeing, but do not perceive.'"

Now it's time to look around. I find palm trees and all sorts of new sounds. Even though I'm on an island, it's relatively big, especially traveling on foot as I spend the rest of the day seeing what I can find.

It can all be so overwhelming when everything is new, but when you are immersed in a new season, you must go forth in faith and confidence. God has called you to a place you've never been before, and growth is always outside of your comfort zone. You have to go to places you've never been to have the success you've never seen. Where ever God calls you, He equips you. God says your steps are ordered and He has predestined your life. Because of this, he must provide for that next step. So walk into the next step with boldness. People may think you don't deserve to be there, but God has placed you there for a reason. You are more than a conqueror and to conquer something you have to go where you've never gone before. Whether it's away from the shore into the deep, or it's a trip into the shadowy jungle, trust that He is with you. "Though I walk through the valley of the shadow of death, I will fear no evil; for you are with me; your rod and your staff, they comfort me" (Psalm 23:4).

FIND HIGH GROUND

Psalm 119:164 (NKJV): "Seven times a day I praise you, because of Your righteous judgments."

I've noticed I have so much peace during the day if I start my day with prayer. It changes my mindset off of me and onto the Lord and what He wants to be accomplished in my life. I found a high point on the island I go to and pray in the morning and during the day. If I don't know what to pray I just open my Bible and proclaim God's words over my life.

God didn't create you for the shadows. He wants to take you higher but to know where God wants you to go; you need to pray. Prayer is essential. Learn to go to God first with all things. Imagine someone having a map of your whole life, and you never talk to them. Seek God for guidance, thanks, praise, and anxiety. Even in the little things. He wants to lead you to higher ground. On the higher ground, you can see where you came from and appreciated it. On the high ground, you can see danger ahead. In the valley, you can't see ahead, but on the mountain, you can see God's glory. Prayer is essential in both places. Prayer brings Gods will on earth as it is in heaven. You have things in the heavenly realm God has for you, and He is waiting on you to have enough faith to pray and ask for them. Prayer is just a conversation between you and God. God talks to you through His word. And the best way to talk to Him is to say His word back to Him. In a conversation, the best way to communicate that you understand what the other person said is to say it back to them. Prayer is one way God speaks to you. "Faith comes by hearing, and hearing by the word of God" (Romans 10:17). Speak back to God.

ADVENTURE

Genesis 12:1–3 (NKJV): "Now the Lord had said to Abram: 'Get out of your country, from your family and your father's house to a land that I will show you. I will make you a great nation; I will bless you and make your name great, and you shall be a blessing. I will bless those who bless you, and I will curse him who curses you.'"

I feel like God is leading me further. Today I took an adventure around parts of the island I haven't been to, and though I didn't see it all, I want to learn more about this island that I'm on.

The best way to get to know a place is to explore. When you're lead by the Lord, He has ordered your steps and made provision for each one. He has already planned your steps, so He has prepared everything you need to make that step and to take the next one. With confidence, then, learn everything about the place you're at—the sand, the trees, the animals, the terrain, and the way of the land. If ministry is where God has called you, learn everything about it, not just where God wants you to be. Learn all the parts of ministry. Learn what it means and learn the different possibilities. If God hasn't called you to vocational ministry, learn how you can use your gifts to impact the kingdom. Learn about people that are in your field or have made a difference for the kingdom of God. Explore deeply on your side of the island but dare to adventure to the other parts of the island as well.

PRAYER

WRITE YOUR OWN HERE

CHAPTER 3

BUILDING A LITTLE STRUCTURE

WAKE UP EARLY

After a long day of exploring, my body wanted to sleep in, but I'm training it to wake up early. I don't want to get caught up in where I'm at right now. I want to make the best out of my situation. I could be lazy and think that I'm on an island so I don't have to do anything, but I want to do my best at everything I put my hands on. It's the spirit of excellence on me. I can get more done when I wake up. I know that this isn't where I'm going to be forever.

You got something accomplished, so now it's time to relax and sleep in, right? Of course not! It's time to start waking up earlier and digging deeper. It's the best way to be the most productive in your day. Your brain functions better in the morning, let's get the most out of it. Completing your biggest to-dos in the morning will make your day easier and more satisfying. You will feel more accomplished.

When you procrastinate, it gets put back later and later, by the time you have to get the task done, your energy is already drained. Also, when you wake up early, you get more daylight. You can explore the island longer and get more goals completed. Prayer and reading your Bible are great ways to start your day, and they give you the wisdom you need to make it through. So wake up early because, the early bird catches the worm.

Tip: Proverbs is a great read in the mornings, it's a quick read and will give you the wisdom to make the decisions you have to make that day. There are 31 proverbs, and you can do one a day, plus one some months.

FIND PROTECTION

Psalm 84:3–4 (NKJV): "Even the sparrow has found a home, And the swallow a nest for herself, where she may lay her young—even Your altars, O

Lord of hosts, My King and my God. Blessed are those who dwell in your house."

Being on an island sounds like all fun and games, rainbows and sunshine, but there is a lot of danger. In the day I am alright, but at night, many of the dangers are not visible. Snakes, spiders, bugs, animals, and even the elements can creep up on you at night. The late-night sounds can be frightening too. The voices in my head get louder. The darkness seems to creep in closer and closer. I toss and turn. It wasn't a comfortable sleep, but I wake up in the morning determined to not go through that again. I need protection from my environment.

No matter how many dangers there are in your environment, there is always protection. What is your covering? Prayer is essential. It may feel selfish or a scary thing to do, but ask for prayer. Pray about it first. Then think about who you can go to when you need prayer—someone you can trust. Someone at your church, small group, leader, mentor, pastor, family, friend, teacher, grandma, or even a person you don't know that has a strong faith.

Find people that will help protect you from the harsh elements of the cold world. The enemy wants you bad. He wants to stop you from reaching the potential God has for you. The enemy wouldn't be attacking you if you didn't have something valuable on the inside of you. Thieves don't break into empty houses. A car doesn't have safety features and air bags to protect the car. The safety features are to protect what's on the inside. You are the car, the vehicle, the vessel for the greatness God has placed inside of you. Find out who your covering is because your covering is your protection.

Prayer: God, I pray you will keep me out of the arena of temptation, keep evil far from me, put a supernatural barrier around me, enlarge my hedge, and encamp your angels around me. Lord watch over me, lead me, and guide me. Show me the people around me that are my covering and those that I am covering and strengthen us. I thank you, Father, for your protection, in Jesus name I pray. Amen.

BUILD SHELTER

Luke 6:47-49 (NKJV): "Whoever comes to me, and hears my sayings and does them, I will show you whom he is like: He is like a man building a house, who dug deep and laid the foundation on the rock. And when the flood arose, the stream beat vehemently against that house, and could not shake it, for it was founded on the rock. But he who heard and did nothing is like a man who built a house on the earth without a foundation, against which the stream beat vehemently; and immediately it fell. And the ruin of that house was great."

After a couple of long nights on the island, I know the importance of protection, so now it's time to build a shelter. It hasn't rained yet, but I'm sure it will. I don't have all the pieces for a shelter, but I have faith. Where am I going to build it though? I can't build on the shore; the sand isn't stable, and I don't want to be unstable. I have to build on solid ground. I've scoped the island out and adventured around. I know a perfect place–an open space surrounded by trees. It's close enough to the shore and has a stream near it.

Have you ever put your faith in something other than the Lord, and a huge wave came and washed it completely away?

KNOW WHEN STORMS ARE COMING

James 1:5-6 (NKJV): "If any of you lacks wisdom, let him ask of God, who gives to all liberally and without reproach, and it will be given to him. But let him ask in faith, with no doubting, for he who doubts is like a wave of the sea driven and tossed by the wind."

The first rain came today, and luckily I was led to build my shelter earlier, or I would have had a bad day. The storm beat against my walls and doubt started to creep in. Some drops got through, but it stood its ground. Next time I will be more prepared. The Bible also warns us that trouble will come and what to do when it comes. I was reading the book of James on the beach earlier, and it says God will give me wisdom.

Storms will come, and if you don't think that's true, those storms will devastate you, so be prepared. It rains on the just and the unjust the same; it's just how you walk through it that makes the difference. Even in the longest storms, don't lose faith. This too shall pass.

Prayer: God, I pray you give me wisdom on when storms are coming and what the schemes of the enemy are so that I can be prepared, in Jesus name. Amen.

FIND WARMTH

Colossians 3:23 (NKJV): "And whatever you do, do it heartily, as to the Lord and not to men."

After the storms came through, the next couple of days were cold and cloudy. It was warmer inside my shelter, but I still needed more warmth. The wind didn't make it any better either, but in the wind, I heard something. I wanted to know what it was, so I went to the high ground, prayed, and on my way down, it hit me-a fire! I went to my shelter and found a jacket from the pile of things I got off the shore. Then I went out and gathered wood and stones.

If you're going to endure, you need to find warmth from inside you–a fire! Something you're passionate about! Something that gets your blood pumping. For example, if you grew up hungry, you might find a fire in ending world hunger. God usually lets you go through something, so that you can help others out of that very thing. It might be a passion the develops from your situation, or you might just be born with it. An example of this might be that you grew up painting and have a passion for art. Whatever your passion is, let it burn bright.

MAKE A FIRE

Luke 3:22 (NKJV): "And the Holy Spirit descended in bodily form like a dove upon Him, and a voice came from heaven which said, 'You are My beloved Son; in You, I am well pleased.'"

Now I have a little warmth and a little fire, but in this next season, I am going to need something greater than that. I am going to need a "fire" fire. Just because I made a fire doesn't mean I'm a fire-starting expert. Because of this, I'm going to need divine wisdom.

Jesus May have spoken or ministered to people growing up; we don't know. But, He didn't start His ministry on earth until He was baptized and the Holy Spirit descended on Him. The disciples didn't start their ministry until the Holy Spirit descended on them. Saul was persecuting Christians until Jesus met him on the road to Damascus. Then he was filled with the Holy Spirit and baptized. Now we know him as Paul, and he is one of the Bible greats. He even wrote several books in the Bible.

You won't be able to do God's work without the Holy Spirit–the one that leads you to all knowledge and truth. John the Baptist said, "I baptize with water, and Jesus came to baptize with fire and the Holy Spirit." Allow the Holy Spirit into every part of your life so you can do all you were destined to do.

Prayer: Lord, I thank you for the Holy Spirit. I thank you for all the things that you have predestined for me and for equipping me with everything I need. Holy Spirit, lead me to wisdom, knowledge, truth, revelation, and discernment. Lead my words, thoughts, and actions. Lord, let it be your will and not mine. In Jesus name. Amen.

KEEP THE FIRE GOING

John 8:12 (NKJV): "Then Jesus spoke to them again, saying, 'I am the light of the world. He who follows me shall not walk in darkness, but have the light of life.'"

Leviticus 6:12-13 (NKJV): "And the fire on the altar shall be kept burning on it; it shall not be put out. And the priest shall burn wood on it every morning, and lay the burnt offering in order on it; and he shall burn on it the fat of the peace offerings. A fire shall always be burning on the altar; it shall never go out."

The next day, after a great victory, I sat on the beach reading the Word of God. I have this newness about me. Time flies when you are reading something so interesting. Before I knew it, it was nighttime, and just because I made a fire yesterday doesn't mean it will burn today. I learned that I have to keep the fire going.

Jesus is the light of the world that shines in you. Jesus is the way to what is truly life, but the scripture refers to those that *follow* Him. If you don't follow Him, you are walking away from the light. It's not a one-time prayer; it's a daily choice. Keep your eyes on Jesus because he is the path that lights your feet. Your fire may burst up, or it may go down a little, but it will never go out. Keep the fire going!

PRAYER

WRITE YOUR OWN HERE

SECTION 2

CHAPTER 4

REALIZE WHAT'S PRECIOUS TO YOU

REALIZE WHAT'S PRECIOUS TO YOU

Matthew 6:19-21 (NKJV): "Do not lay up for yourselves treasures on earth, where moth and rust destroy and where thieves break in and steal; but lay up for yourselves treasures in heaven, where neither moth nor rust destroys and where thieves do not break in and steal. For where your treasure is, there your heart will also be."

In my life, I've felt like there were times when I had it all and times when I felt like I had nothing. Being on an island and all that I was used to being taken away makes me realize what matters. I'm thinking about all the time and energy I've wasted on meaningless things. All the hours sitting and scrolling down my social media feed or binge-watching television shows. Pointless arguments and going places to impress people that didn't care about me. Ignoring the people that needed me and that were there for me. Buying new shoes instead of buying someone close to me something they needed. If I had another chance, I would cherish the things that matter.

What matters to you? What do you care about? What do you value? Do you give these things the right attention and time they deserve?

REMEMBER WHO YOU LOVE

Today, my family, my friends, and everyone I know back home were on my mind heavy. I know they are worried about me. I want to get off the island for them. They give me hope and a reason to push on when sometimes I don't want to. I'm also thinking about the people I haven't met yet because they need to hear my story as well.

When times get rough, you have to remember who you are doing this for. First and foremost, you should do it for the Lord. You want to please your Father, and you love Him. If you love God, then you will love His people. There will be times when you don't want to do it for yourself. In these times, keep people in mind that you are doing it for because it's bigger than you.

Sometimes you have to do it for yourself because you don't want to do it for people. You can be mad at your boss, or someone has done you wrong. That's when your love for God and your spirit of excellence work best. In every season, find that reason that's bigger than you and is why you're pushing on. Consider these questions to ask yourself: Am I doing it out of the kindness of my heart? Am I doing it for selfish reasons? Does my love for the creator help me love the creation? Am I doing everything I put my hands to with excellence? Why or why not? Who do you love? Use that love to motivate you.

DON'T FORGET THE LITTLE THINGS

Today, I was looking through some stuff, and I found my favorite bracelet. Back home, it meant a lot to me. Because of all that happened and being on the island, I had forgotten about it. Finding that made me slow down and remember the little details of life. Sometimes it's the little things in moments of our lives that can seem so big.

Sometimes life can be going so fast, and you can be overwhelmed with the new thing. You can have big things on your plate, but it's the little things that helped you to get to this point. Imagine you are going on the interstate going 90 mph. At that speed, you better be focused on what's ahead of you. Then you get a flat tire. Something like that slows everything down. Now you see things that you didn't see before. You can see the beautiful scenery. You can see the actual size of the lines on the road. You can notice the details. You also see how fast other cars are going.

When you were going fast, you didn't notice how fast the other cars were going because you were going at the same pace. A flat tire is a time to slow everything down and assess what happened. It's a time to reflect and then plan for when you get back on the road. This time it's important to pay attention to the little things. Success is a bunch of little things

done right over and over. It's like building a Lego
island; you have to do it piece by piece.

PRAYER

WRITE YOUR OWN HERE

CHAPTER 5

TIME TO EAT

HUNT

Matthew 7:7 (NKJV) "Ask, and it will be given to you, seek, and you will find."

I woke up this morning, and I didn't start my day with the best news. I went into my food stash, and it was really low. I should have planned and thought into the future. I knew it wouldn't last forever, but I didn't think ahead about what I would do when it ran out.

Have you ever prayed to God for something and expected the clouds to part and the thing you prayed for to fall from heaven? It sounds crazy, but all too often we say that with our actions. When you pray for something, you have to go into hunting mode. That means constantly looking for it, preparing for it, and going to get it. That could also mean getting in position for it because it could come to you. The bottom line is that you have to be ready for it.

I'm from Tennessee, but if you're not, bear with me. A hunter doesn't just go out into the woods with no gun, looking at flowers, and planning to go sleep in a tree. He has faith that he is going to catch a deer. He is looking for it and is prepared for when he sees one. (If he is from Kentucky, he might be sleeping in the tree.) It's not all about works; you need faith. You show your faith by your works. You should be hunting for anything that is about God. Whether it be a church, seeing scriptures, God moments, or a chance to see or participate in what God is doing on Earth. Don't just wonder or you'll get lost. Hunt down your blessings. (If you're from Kentucky, don't take it to heart; I will try to fit in an Alabama joke too.)

FOOD

John 4:34 (NKJV): Jesus said to them, "My food is to do the will of Him who sent me, and to finish His work."

OPEN YOUR EYES, AND YOU WILL BE SATISFIED WITH BREAD

Today, I went into full hunter mode. I set traps, made sharp spears, and even made some camouflage. I found some good spots where there were many wild animal tracks. I didn't catch anything big, but for day one a rabbit is a win. I also got a few bugs, high in protein, to eat as a little appetizer. They're gross, but you've got to do what you've got to do. This experience has helped me grow. I'm trying to do things I've never done and experience results I've never seen before.

Jesus said that His food is to do the will of the Father. How hungry are you? God didn't send His son to save you so you can just chill and get a "get into heaven free" card. He chose you so that you can complete His will on Earth. God has plans for good, and they involve you. Your purpose is to be the light on Earth and to be an ambassador for Him, do His work, save souls, and be a willing vessel for Him with the help of the Holy Spirit.

Earthly food and material things will perish, but God has given you eternal life. Remember, "Faith comes by hearing and hearing by the word of God" (Romans 10:17). It's essential to read the Bible. Not just for you, but so you can lead others to do the same. His word is life and food to your bones. How many people are you helping experience the same thing?

THERE ARE PLENTY OF FISH

Mark 1:17 (NKJV): "Then Jesus said to them, 'Follow Me, and I will make you become fishers of men.'"

After a week of hard work and hunting, I got a revelation. I realized that I'm on an island and there are plenty of fish. My first-day fishing, I caught a weeks' worth of food. It was way easier than trying to catch big animals. I didn't give up on the hunt, but this is just a different type of hunt. Just like hunting the wild animals, some days I caught a lot of fish and some days I didn't catch anything. Through it all, I never got discouraged.

As Christ followers, we are called to spread the gospel and lead others to Christ. Some days it will be easy, and some days it will be hard. The good news is the results are in God's hands. He is the one that calls. He is the only one that has the power to save. God said to Samuel in 1 Samuel 8:7, "For they have not rejected you, but they have rejected me, that I should not reign over them." It's not how we do it; we just have to be willing vessels. God will choose and call as He pleases by the power of the Holy Spirit.

Sometimes we think we chose God, but before He created the earth, He chose you. One day He opened your eyes so you could see the truth and opened your ears so you could hear His voice. There are plenty of fish. Start with the people around you—your family, your friends, and your coworkers. Then you can tell the people you meet at the gym, at the store, and everywhere you go.

HARVEST

Proverbs 11:24–25 (NKJV): "There is one who scatters, yet increases more; and there is one who withholds more than is right, but it leads to poverty. The generous soul will be made rich, and he who waters will also be watered himself."

All my hard work paid off, but it was a struggle. I had to keep reminding myself that it would be worth it. Now I have plenty of food to last me a while. It is a blessing from above. Today, I fasted and spent my day in the Bible. In it, I read about sacrifices to the Lord. I was hungry, but I was hungrier for God. I was tired of my hard work, but I put the Lord before my desires, giving Him the time He deserved. I could never repay Him, but I will give Him all I have.

Sowing and reaping is a principle from the beginning of time and is still true today. You reap what you sow. Most of the time, you reap more than what you sowed. In a sowing season, it's difficult because you don't always see the fruit. Your reward in the end, however, will be worth it so push through. When you are in a sowing season, go into grind mode and give everything you have to anything you put your hand to. Those that are faithful over a little will be given much.

God isn't worried about things; He is worried about you. He wants to mold you, give you integrity, make you responsible, grow you, and instill things into you so that when He blesses you, the blessings don't overtake you. Too much of a good thing can still destroy you. The hard work molds your character and gives you wisdom so when He gives you more, you know what to do with it. A sowing season stretches your faith because you can't see your reward yet, so when it shows up, you praise Him and Him alone. Then He stretches your faith even more. He asks you to give the first fruits of all your increases to Him. You may feel like, "I worked hard for this" or "What if this or that happens, and I don't have enough," but God says that your reward for giving to Him will be tenfold. If you sow right, the blessings are abundant. You receive a harvest, wisdom, integrity, and another blessing for being obedient. Trust in God, and He will bless you.

PRAYER

WRITE YOUR OWN HERE

CHAPTER 6

GET FAMILIAR

_____

FIND SOME SHADE

Proverbs 10:4–5 (NKJV): "He who has a slack hand becomes poor, but the hand of the diligent makes rich. He who gathers in summer is a wise son; he who sleeps in harvest is a son who causes shame."

I woke up this morning and had a crazy thought— I was starting to like this place. It's not the image I had of long summer days, a cool breeze, and warm sand between my toes, but through this experience, I've grown so much. I read my Bible till midday this morning, in Genesis, it talked about creation. I feel like I'm creating something here. God created Adam and Eve for intimacy, so

I thought if that what the purpose of them being created then He wants intimacy with me also. Soon after I finished reading, the sun was out and it was kind of warm, so I sat under a tree and talked to God. I heard a voice say, "Get some rest," and I started to doze off.

Let's not be lazy. We should do everything with excellence. After our work is done well, then we should rest. God created us to rest. Use rest as a weapon. It helps refresh and rejuvenate us. Even doing too much of something good can be bad. Don't run yourself until you burnout because this life is a marathon, not a sprint. Get some rest for the things ahead.

MAKE YOUR WAY INLAND

Ephesians 5:15–17 (NKJV): "See then that you walk circumspectly, not as fools but as wise, redeeming the time because the days are evil. therefore do not be unwise, but understand what the will of the Lord is."

Today I wanted to explore a little more of the island, something I haven't done since my last adventure. I can't let fear of the unknown hold me back.

Again, God is calling you deeper. He doesn't want you to stay where you're at. He wants to grow you and growth comes from outside your comfort zone and from a place of unfamiliarity. You can't stay where you are because He has greater for you, and that greater place is in the thick of things. There is an outer call and an inner call. An outer call is when someone tells you about the gospel, someone tells you about Jesus, or when you hear the Word of God. You might have heard it before, but this time it was different. This time you were ready to receive.

KNOW THE ANIMAL LIFE

1 Peter 5:8 (NKJV): "Be sober, be vigilant; because your adversary the devil walks about like a roaring lion, seeking whom he may devour."

As I went deeper into the island, I saw many different animals I had never seen including a fierce beast from afar. I have to be more watchful and be aware of my environment. I also saw beautiful animals as well, and some of them came close enough for me to touch.

As Christ followers, we have to be aware. There is an enemy seeking to kill us, and he isn't alone either. There are wolves in sheep's clothing. They look sweet but come to devour you when your guard is down. The Bible says many will be deceived and false prophets will arise in the end. How do we know the difference between them all? We will know the difference by their fruit. God has sent us the Holy Spirit to give us discernment. God said His sheep would know His voice. The sheep are your brothers and sisters in Christ. Look out for them, and make sure they are not deceived and devoured.

PRAYER

WRITE YOUR OWN HERE

SECTION 3

CHAPTER 7

ABUNDANT WATER

FIND A WELL

John 4:7–14 (NKJV): "A woman of Samaria came to draw water. Jesus said to her, 'Give Me a drink.' For His disciples had gone away into the city to buy food. Then the woman of Samaria said to Him, 'How is it that you, being a Jew, ask a drink from me, a Samaritan woman?' For Jews have no dealings with Samaritans. Jesus answered and said to her, 'If you knew the gift of God, and who it is who says to you, 'Give Me a drink,' you would have asked Him, and He would have given you living water.' The woman said to Him, 'Sir, you have nothing to draw with, and the well is deep. Where then do you get that living water? Are you greater than our father Jacob, who gave us the well, and drank from it himself, as well as his sons and his livestock?' Jesus answered and said to her, 'Whoever drinks of this water will thirst again, but whoever drinks of the water that I shall give him will never thirst. But the water that I shall give him will become in him a fountain of water springing up into everlasting life.'"

While I was inland, I found a spring. Fresh water was pouring out. I'm glad I didn't let fear hold me back. The trip was worth it because now I don't have to worry about my water situation. Coconuts are good, but getting into it is a pain.

Jesus is our well, our spring, and the quencher of our thirst. He is our everlasting water, and with him we shall never thirst again. Run to Jesus and have everlasting life. He is our supply, and he is enough. Don't be selfish because He is enough for everybody. Just like the woman in this story, once you get a taste, you will want to run and tell everyone you know.

CLEAN WATER SYSTEM

1 Timothy 6:17–19 (NKJV): "Command those who are rich in this present age not to be haughty, nor to trust in uncertain riches but in the living God, who gives us richly all things to enjoy. Let them do good that they be rich in good works, ready to give, willing to share, storing up for themselves a good foundation for the time to come, that they may lay hold on eternal life."

Today I made a clean water system that purifies water from the spring I discovered by removing anything bad from the water that I need.

Jesus is our everlasting water and our eternal life, but that doesn't stop us from wanting other things. Jesus should be your deepest desire, but that doesn't mean He doesn't want you to have things. He just doesn't want things to have you. Don't love the gift more than the giver. The word of God is our filter that tells us what is edifying and what is not. It tells us how to be rich in good works, how to live a Godly life, and how to use the resources we have been given. Thank the Lord for every perfect gift from above.

PRAYER

WRITE YOUR OWN HERE

CHAPTER 8

WATCH OUT

STAY AWAY FROM DEAD PLACES

Matthew 27:7–8 (NKJV): "And they consulted together and bought with them the potter's field, to bury strangers in. Therefore that field has been called the Field of Blood to this day."

Today, I wandered upon a part of the island that was horrific. There were bones and scavengers everywhere. Not much had grown there, it didn't get much sunlight, and the smell was terrible. I made a note to myself not to go back there ever again.

There are places we can go in our lives that are dead places. We can be lured there by friends, an idea of fun, or we may just end up there at these places that are spiritually dead. There are bones there because many have lost their lives (spiritually, physically, and mentally). Stay away from these dead places that drain you and don't have light.

WATCH FOR TRAPS

Psalm 141:9 (NKJV) "Keep me from the snares they have laid for me, and from the traps of the workers of iniquity."

Upon leaving the dead place, there were many traps. It's like it didn't want me to leave until harm occurred. I barely made it out alive.

In life, there will be many traps. The Bible describes the devil like a lion looking to devour. He comes to kill, steal, and destroy. He doesn't want you to leave until you are ensnared by his traps. A seductress woman's lips are like honey, but her feet lead to hell. You will have many opportunities to be offended, and evil will constantly tempt you, but the road to hell is broad, and there are many ways to it. Watch for traps, be aware, and stay away.

DON'T BE AFRAID OF THE WAVES

Matthew 14:28–32 (NKJV): "And Peter answered Him and said, 'Lord, if it is you, command me to come to You on the water.' So He said, 'Come.' And when Peter had come down out of the boat, he walked on water to go to Jesus. But when he saw that the wind was boisterous, he was afraid; and beginning to sink he cried out, saying, 'Lord, save me!' And immediately Jesus stretched out His hand and caught him, and said to him, 'O you of little faith, why did you doubt?' And when they got into the boat, the wind ceased."

When I fish, I try to stay near the shore, but it seems like the further I go, the bigger the fish are.

Jesus is calling you deeper and further than you've ever gone before. He hasn't called you so you can stay where you're at. He wants to take you to depths you've never been before. He wants to do great works through you. First, however, you have to yield yourself to His Lordship and understand that it's bigger than you.

God wants to use you to further His purposes on Earth, and there are people out there that need you. The waves may seem big, the thing He has called you to do may seem too big for you, but Jesus calms the storms, commands the waves, and tells the wind which way to go. He is in control. Wherever He brings you, He equips you. Go further and further away from the shore and trust in the Lord. Believe you can walk on water because He called you onto the water. When your faith is low, the Lord will stick out His hand and save you, so walk on water with confidence and boldness. There is a great reward that is to be had when risking it all for Jesus–on Earth and in Heaven.

PRAYER

WRITE YOUR OWN HERE

CHAPTER 9

LONG SUFFERING

SOME STUFF GETS REAL

2 Corinthians 4:16-18 (NKJV): "Therefore we do not lose heart. Even though our outward man is perishing, yet the inward man is renewed day by day. For our light affliction, which is but for a moment, is working for us a far more exceeding and eternal weight of glory, while we do not look at the things which are seen, but at the things which are not seen. For the things which are seen are temporary, but the things which are not seen are eternal."

This week has been rough. Storms have come every day, I haven't caught any food, and the sun *hasn't shown its face much. My faith has been tested, and I've called out to God, but I feel like I've gotten no answer. A tree fell on my shelter, but because of that, I added new pieces to it, and it was better than before. When the storms slowed down a few days later, I decided that I would no longer take sunny days for granted. The storms strengthened my trust in God and also my faith that He will bring me through.*

We all go through storms, but I feel like when we preach the gospel, we often times leave out the part about long suffering–the fact that we will suffer for the name of Jesus. We will suffer for Christ's sake. It's through this suffering that God matures us for what He has for us later. This process of maturing is important because only then can He give you more because only then will you have the wisdom and maturity to know how to handle it. This maturity is both physical and spiritual. The process of physical maturity is for what God has for you on Earth while the process of spiritual maturity is for what God has for you in heaven.

Similarly, sanctification is becoming more like Jesus every day. Anytime you are being matured in life it isn't pleasant. God is growing you and preparing you for what He has for you in heaven, so He gives you tests to grow you. God is pruning you and cutting out what doesn't need to be there. God uses storms to make you better. Storms take out what's dead in your life.

In a storm, don't blame God, complain, or lose sight of what God has for you. God loves you, but He still prunes you. Storms make us spiritually mature. They strengthen our inner man. It rains on the just and the unjust the same; it's how you walk through it that makes the difference. It's a mindset. Do you trust God? See storms as valuable. Think of them like you can get something out of them.

What is God doing in this storm? Know that you are supposed to be there. Don't lose your peace, joy, and momentum while in the storm. God is keeping you. Storms equal spiritual maturity. Spiritual maturity equals value. Tests equal trust, and trust turns into faith.

God, I have faith that you will bring me through this storm because you are the same God that brought me out of the last one. Have faith in God's wisdom. Lord, though you slay me, yet will I trust you.

Read John 15 to see what Jesus has to say.

KEEP AWAY FROM DANGER!

Psalms 38:12 (NKJV): "Those also who seek my life lay snares for me; those who seek my hurt speak of destruction, and plan deception all the day long."

This feels like a stormy season. The storms have lessened in intensity but have yet to cease completely. The storms have altered the paths, so today I had to go near the dead place, but I kept as far away as possible.

When you are speaking truth, when you are doing good, when you are helping others, you would think people would love you, accept you, and protect you as one of their own. Jesus was a Jew born to His people. He did great works, healing, teaching, and loving, but He was not accepted by His people. The religious people at that time were infatuated with the coming of the Messiah. They knew the prophecies, and they knew the Word. You would think if the Lord came down, at least the religious people would love Him, but they killed Him.

We are called to suffer for Jesus name. We may not be killed, but people are plotting against us. Be aware. Do not back down, but stay cautious while at the same time knowing we are called to be light in the darkness. That means we are going to be surrounded by darkness. The darkness wants to defeat you. Stay away from the traps people have laid before you. Many times the people asked Jesus questions to trap Him. Many times they tried to trap Daniel. If you are doing God's work, remember there is an adversary.

ENDURE THE STORMS

Philippians 4:11-13 (NKJV): "Not that I speak in regard to need, for I have learned in whatever state I am, to be content: I know how to be abased, and I know how to abound. Everywhere and in all things I have learned both to be full and to be hungry, both to abound and to suffer need. I can do all things through Christ who strengthens me."

The storms have yet to stop. God is stretching the faith I gained from the first storms. Power from above is keeping me. I know this because it is not my strength. Peace and joy I couldn't muster up on my own. I trust in the Lord that I will make it through these storms too.

77

God loves you enough not to keep you where you are at. He is constantly stretching you with life of tests. Through them, you are blessed. James said have joy. Trials produce endurance and patience, so you can be lacking nothing in the end. Read James 1. The storms help you produce contentment, so that whether in a valley or on a mountain, you will have praise on your tongue. This too shall pass.

KEEP THE FAITH

Romans 8:28 (NKJV): "And we know that all things work together for good to those who love God, to those who are the called according to His purpose."

I know that if I give up faith, I will give up hope. I don't plan on dying on this island. I plan on living beyond this island. This isn't my home. My prayer is for God to deliver me and I have faith in that.

Keep the faith, knowing that your brothers and sisters around the world are enduring hardships. Know that God has had a plan for you since the beginning. His plan works out for the good of those that love Him. In every storm, there is a lesson. It is all for your betterment. Keep the faith. It is by faith, you believe in Jesus. It is by faith, you receive blessings, grace, and favor. Faith is an action. The more you grow in the knowledge of God, the more you act on faith no matter what you're going through, no matter the situation. In Daniel 3, they trusted and had faith that if God delivered or didn't deliver it will be a favorable outcome. Is there doubt in faith? Without a doubt, there is no need for faith. Most times the doubt isn't in God but the outcome. Faith is built over experiences. This is obedience. Don't lose faith in God Almighty. If you lose faith, you lose all hope. You will lose everything. Keep the faith!

KEEP YOUR STRENGTH

Psalm 84:5 (NKJV) "Blessed is the man whose strength is in You, whose heart is set on pilgrimage."

I feel tired and weary. I don't know how much longer I can go. I pray to God for a glimmer of hope. He blesses me with strength. I make it through the day. The funny thing is as I look back on it I've gotten a lot done during these storms-

mentally and on the island. The lesson I learned is that my strength comes from the Lord.

Every perfect gift is from above. All good things come from God, and He knows your needs. If you ask your earthly father for bread, does he give you a stone? So how much more will your Father who is in heaven give you good things if you ask Him? Call out to the one who can supply for your needs. He can give you strength to endure.

MAKE A FRIEND

Ecclesiastes 4:9-12 (NKJV): "Two are better than one because they have a good reward for their labour. For if they fall, one will lift his companion. But woe to him who is alone when he falls, for he has no one to help him up. Again, if two lies down together, they will keep warm; but how can one be warm alone? Though one may be overpowered by another, two can withstand him. And a threefold cord is not quickly broken."

One of the hardest things about being on this island is being here alone. I feel like I need someone to talk to-someone to spill everything out too or someone I know is there and cares, even if they don't have the answer... Today, I met Casey-my coconut friend. Everything changed when I met him. He took me out of the place I was in, and since our meeting, it's been nothing but sunshine.

FELLOWSHIP

Proverbs 17:17 (NKJV): "A friend loves at all times, and a brother is born for adversity."

Fellowship is key. The Church is Jesus's bride, and if we love Jesus, we love His Church. The people you fellowship with help you grow and are there through the good, the bad, and the ugly. They protect you, pray for you, and celebrate you. They uplift and encourage you but also challenge you. The enemy wants you alone. That's when you are most vulnerable. When I asked my mentors and elders how not to backslide, lose the fire, or lose the faith, they said, "Fellowship is essential. They are there, so you don't fall."

PRAYER

WRITE YOUR OWN HERE

SECTION 4

CHAPTER 10

IT'S BIGGER THAN THE ISLAND

KEEP TRACK OF TIME

Ecclesiastes 3:1-11 (NKJV): "To everything there is a season, a time for every purpose under heaven: a time to be born, and a time to die; a time to plant, and a time to pluck what is planted; a time to kill, and a time to heal; a time to break down, and a time to build up; a time to weep, and a time to laugh; a time to mourn, and a time to dance; a time to cast away stones, and a time to gather stones; a time to embrace, and a time to refrain from embracing; a time to gain, and a time to lose; a time to keep, and a time to throw away; a time to tear, and a time to sew; a time to keep silence, and a time to speak; a time to love, and a time to hate; a time of war, and a time of peace. What profit has the worker from that in which he labors? I have seen the God-given task with which the sons of men are to be occupied. He has made everything beautiful in its time. Also, He has put eternity in their hearts, except that no one can find out the work that God does from beginning to end."

One thing I've learned while on the island is to learn how to keep track of time. When I leave for a trip inland, I have to have a sense of time. If I don't, I can take a long trip and not account for the time needed to make it back which would cause me to get stuck in the dark and easily lost. I have to know the time and pace myself accordingly.

God made seasons for a reason. Everything has its perfect time, and everything is made perfect in time, including you. You have to be aware of this and know what type of season you are in. You can be moving along well, but if it's not the right time, your time could go to waste. Wifi is great, but what use would it have 100 years ago? Be led by the Spirit and ask God what He wants you to accomplish in this season. What season is this? What has God called for me to do in this season? What do I need to focus on in this season? Get the most out of this season. There is always going to be scarcity, but work with what you have. Those that are faithful with little can be trusted with much.

SUNRISE

Genesis 1:5 (NKJV): "God called the light Day, and the darkness He called Night. So the evening and the morning were the first days."

I thought on an island that my days would be relaxing, sleeping in, and enjoying life on a beach. I've learned quickly, however, that to get the most out of my day, I needed to wake up close to sunrise. Back home, I have rarely seen or paid attention to a sunrise. On the island, sunrises have been one of my favorite things. The symbolism is amazing. It reminds me that it's a new day. All the things of yesterday have passed away, and today all things are new. Each day is a new beginning. I can't take back what I did yesterday, but I can control what I do today.

The sunrise is a great symbolism for the start of something new. Every day, wake up and thank God for a new start and another day to reach higher and to make a difference. This can be a new habit, project, or just a new attitude. Keep growing, keep aspiring for better, keep learning, and make the most of this day God has given you.

Prayer: Lord I thank you for the sunrise. Lord, I praise you. Your mercy, grace, and favor are new each day. I thank you for your Son, my savior, because of His blood I am washed clean and made new. I am sanctified through Christ. Lord help me to remember to notice the little things because you have created even the smallest things for a purpose.

SUNSET

Genesis 1:5 (NKJV): "God called the light Day, and the darkness He called Night. So the evening and the morning were the first days."

Keeping track of the sunset is just as important. Like I've said before, I'm not trying to get stuck inland when the sun is setting. Knowing when the sun sets helps me prepare for the night. It's a great time to look at what I've gotten accomplished today and what I'll need to get done tomorrow. How did I do with the time that was given to me today? Was I effective and efficient? What can I do tomorrow to get the most out of it? Sunset also means to me that it's a time to relax, to lay down all the stress and burdens the day has put on me, and to give them to God. Knowing He is in control of it all.

The night is a tricky time. It's time to relax and release, review and recap how the day went, but overall, give it all to God. You have planted your seeds, and God is the one that waters those seed. Don't let what you didn't do overwhelm you. Clear your mind. It's a great time to talk to God. It's also a great time to read some books about things you enjoy, so light a candle, reflect and release.

TIDE

Proverbs 8:29 (NKJV): "...He assigned to the sea its limit so that the waters would not transgress His command..."

The tide is another thing to keep track of. High and low tide have big effects on everything on the island. Just like there are seasons for everything, the tide is like a daily change. There is a time and a place for everything in a day. I wouldn't want to start working at night time. Timing is everything. The tide happens by gravitational pull.

If you are in Christ, you have the Holy Spirit, and He has a pull too. The Holy Spirit leads you and guides you. When He is tugging you, it's divine timing. Are you looking for that pull or tug from the Holy Spirit throughout your day?

Prayer: Holy Spirit let me become sensitive to your voice. Lead and guide my words, my thoughts, and my actions. Lead me to wisdom, knowledge, truth, discernment, and revelation. In Jesus name, I pray, Amen.

PRAYER

WRITE YOUR OWN HERE

CHAPTER 11

GOOD STEWARD

SAVAGE

This week I plan to create a dining area-place outside the shelter that is covered. I also want to have a covered fire pit area, so if rain comes, it won't put out the fire. I want to make a table to eat on and decorate the dining area with things from the island-maybe some rocks to make the fire pit, plants, and more. I'll use whatever I can find.

USE YOUR RESOURCES

God wants you to be effective with what you have. If you are faithful over little, He can give you much. If you are faithful with what He gives you on Earth, He can give you much in heaven. Most of the time, however, we don't realize how much He has given us. Most of the time, we are looking for finances, but the provision, resources, and people can be more useful than money at times. If you need a house built and you have a friend that has the resources and builds houses for free, wouldn't that be worth more than money? God has put people in your life for a reason. God has given you and the people around you skill sets to help each other succeed. With God all things are possible. Use all the resources given to you.

STORAGE SYSTEMS

This week I wanted to create a storage system, so I can store and organize things. I want to spend a couple of days organizing and a couple days creating a system. This way things don't get lost, and I can easily find them.

Organization is essential, but it isn't a one-time thing; it is something you have to continually work on, so it's good to have a system in place to follow and to continually make that system better. Most of the time, I put things in the same place, so I can always know where it is. A planner or journal are great tools also. You remember more when you write things down. Find what works best for you, but an organized life is better than a cluttered life. Your outside reality may resemble your inside reality. This means that if your room is a wreck, your mind might be in the same state. Clarity is great because you have to have a clear vision about where you are going, and if your life is cluttered, it's hard to know where anything is.

I'd Rather Be On An Island

PRAYER

WRITE YOUR OWN HERE

96

CHAPTER 12

THE JOURNEY

DON'T GET COMFORTABLE
WHERE YOU'RE AT

After everything that I've done, it would be easy to get comfortable. That isn't the case with me though. My hope is to get off this island.

Towards the end of a season, it can be easy to get comfortable. It's easy to get used to how things are in this season. Remember, however, growth comes from outside your comfort zone. Now that you have gotten everything out of this season, God might be waiting for you to make another leap of faith. I wouldn't do this without the voice of God leading you. Sometimes we can get so comfortable in a season we get stuck there, but God wants you to continuously grow, especially when you become too comfortable where you are. We go from glory to glory, and God has more for you, so be content in every season but not complacent.

DON'T DROWN

James 1:6 (NKJV): "But let him ask in faith, with no doubting, for he who doubts is like a wave of the sea driven and tossed by the wind."

Today I lost my cool. I didn't speak to Casey, and for a moment, it felt like I lost all hope. I didn't lose hope, though, because I never lost faith. The entire time I've been here, I had faith that I would get off this island, and I consistently fought doubt, but today I sat in doubt way too long. I let it slowly creep up on me until I was overtaken, so I went to the water and just started swimming out. I was fed up. I thought that I was going to swim until I was found, or I would just swim until I couldn't swim anymore. I didn't get too far out before the waves got rough. I tried to swim back, but the current was bringing me further out, and I started to go under. By the grace of God, however, I got a second wind of energy and made it back to shore exhausted and beat.

DON'T LOSE YOUR COOL

We all have those days where it seems like all hope is lost. In those moments, it's easy to make bad decisions, but don't lose your cool. As my favorite artist, Lauren Daigle says, "When you don't move the mountains I need you to move, when you don't part the waters I wish I could walk through, when you don't give the answers as I cry out to you, I will trust in you." Continue to look to God, cry out to Him, and if He doesn't give you an answer right away, trust Him anyway. Don't get angry with God or others for your situation because God will deliver you. Don't speak negatively during or about the situation. It's how you walk through a trial that matters. We all go through them. It rains on the just and the unjust the same; it's just how you walk through it that makes the difference. Remember, people are watching. They want to know if that faith you say you have is real. When you walk through a trial and keep your faith, God gets the glory when you get delivered.

ASK QUESTIONS

Luke 2:46-47 (NKJV): "Now so it was that after three days they found Him in the temple, sitting in the midst of the teachers, both listening to them and asking them questions. And all who heard Him were astonished at His understanding and answers."

Today, I took time to reflect on my time on the island. I have learned a lot, I have had moments of joy and celebration, my faith is on another level, and I'm thankful for this time to get closer to God and to know God. I asked questions about why I am here. What does God want me to learn? Who am I? What is my purpose? And I believe I found that. Whatever God puts in my hands to do, I want to do it with excellence. In the valleys or on the mountain, I want to do everything for the glory of God.

It's important to ask questions. Why am I here? What is God trying to get out of me? In every struggle, there is a blessing. In every season, there are places God wants you to grow. There are new questions in every season as well. God, what do you want me to focus on in this season? Look for recurring themes and confirmations. Asking questions helps you get understanding. Ask God, mentors, people close to you, or even new people in your life. Get the most out of every season.

It's also important that you don't forget what you learn in a season because you will need it. If you use the things you've learned in previous seasons, it will help you in the upcoming seasons. It may even quicken the season. There is going to be times where you think, "Why me?" You did nothing to get here, and you didn't do anything wrong. Ask why did it happened: "What can I learn?" Asking questions brings deeper revelation. Whether from scripture, life, or a conversation, asking questions can help you get more information. Now that you have the information, ask for understanding and wisdom.

BE ABLE TO ADAPT

Proverbs 3:5–6 (NKJV): "Trust in the Lord with all your heart, and lean not on your understanding; in all your ways acknowledge Him, and He shall direct your paths."

Being on this island, I have had to adapt in many ways–sometimes big and sometimes small. I have had to change my sleep habits and work habits. My environment has changed, so I had to adapt to the place where I've been placed. My influences have changed as well. What moves me here wouldn't move me back home. I didn't have to work for my food; I could just go down the street, and there were food places at every corner. I worked for the money to pay for it, but there wasn't a direct correlation in my mind. I thought my job was to make me happy and was something to fulfill me. Here I haven't had the same tools and utilities. Here on the island, I have had to use what was around me. My influences have changed. God has many instruments of change, and on an island, they may be different than the ones he uses in an urban city.

God has a plan for you, and it doesn't always line up with the way you thought it would. Trust in the creator of all things. No matter where you are, be a servant at heart. Jesus came as a servant and no servant is greater than there master. If you are called to preach to thousands or to pick up a thousand chairs, do it for the glory of God. One day you might be doing one, and the next you might be doing the other. Let God use you wherever and in whatever way He pleases. Be a willing vessel, and you never know where God will take you.

NIGHTTIME RITUALS

Luke 6:12 (NKJV): "Now it came to pass in those days that He went out to the mountain to pray, and continued all night in prayer to God."

During my time here, I have built some great habits. At night, no matter how I feel or what happened that day, I always do these things. I always spend time in prayer and talk to God about how I feel, what happened that day, giving thanks, and talking about what I need and want in the future. I sit around the fire and think about all the possibilities, I plan out what I need for tomorrow, and I also speak positive things over me and my life. I try to end my day with the positives. That's how I like to go to sleep. As you can tell, I wasn't too fond of writing in my journal at first, but now it's a stress reliever for me, and I do this at night also.

Like I've said, there is a time for everything, and I believe nighttime is a great time for your routines and rituals. Whatever that may be, try to make it consistent–things you do at night no matter what.

An example would be setting out your clothes for the next day or setting your keys and wallet next to the door and always in the same place. You want to create a nighttime routine that helps you get ready for the day ahead. I'm a nighttime reader, so I try to set out time to read the Bible and read a personal growth book. Whatever you prefer, you always want to end the day on a positive note. Whatever that routine looks like for you, don't make it binding because then it's a burden; just make it consistent.

HAVE FUN

Psalm 34:1 (NKJV): "I will bless the Lord at all times; His praise shall continually be in my mouth."

I feel like during my time here, I've been a little too stressed and too serious about everything.

Lately, though, I have been letting loose, not in the things I need to get done but in my attitude. Even if He doesn't deliver me from this island, my hope is still in Him. I can't stress my whole life away. I have given it to God. It's in His hands, and truthfully, it's always been in His hands. I have just grown to trust that. Life is much better when you're having fun.

Life is truly much better when you give it all to Him. You are free, so live freely. God doesn't want it to be hard on you; we tend to make it hard on ourselves. Relax and let loose sometimes. It's not that you let everything go but rather that you live your life freely in Christ. Have fun, have peace, praise God, and find joy in all things.

HAVE CELEBRATIONS

Psalm 118:24 (NKJV): "This is the day the Lord has made; we will rejoice and be glad in it."

Today I had a celebration. I spent all day praising God and preparing a feast. I invited Casey, and I gathered a bunch of wood so that I can make a bigger fire tonight that burns for a long time. It was great. My soul and spirit were at peace. My mind wasn't worried about anything because God is so good. The celebration was for all the good God has done and will do. Glory to God and let praises be on my tongue for all my days. Let's make every day a celebration.

In the Bible, there are many celebrations, so don't be over-righteous; celebrate. God has done so much in our lives that if He never did another thing, He has already done more than enough. Bless Him for that. People should question why you have so much joy. Live in that overflow of God's abundant goodness. Oh, the goodness of the Lord. He has saved us from the mud and clay. He has given us abundant life. He has showered you in His love, and one day you will be in His presence. Don't wait until that day though. Let your life be a song, singing the praises of the Lord. Let every day be a celebration.

REVELATION

Today, I thought I was seeing things, but it was Captain Jesus walking up to me. I was overjoyed and ran up to Him and hugged Him like I had never hugged anybody in my life. He said to me that He loved me and that He was always there. He left the briefcase for me. He called me deeper inland. He was the one that left the cross for me and heard my cries. He read my prayer notebook every night while I was asleep. He was the one that called me deeper. When I was worried about my shelter, He stood guard every night and watched over me. He was the one that whispered "make a fire" when I was cold. When the fire was going out, He put more wood on it. The day I found my bracelet, He left it there to remind me about what's precious to me and not to forget the little things. When I set traps, He placed animals in them so I could eat. Before I went out to fish in the mornings, He threw out bait so the fish would be in the spot I went fishing. When I was tired, He was the voice that said, "Get some rest." He continued to call me deeper. He made a path away from the dead places. He threw the bait out further and further away from the shore to grow my faith. He answered my prayers. He held my head above the waves when I passed out and *almost drowned. He said that there is another boat on the other side of the island, and it's time to go home. He is my deliverer.*

I woke up on the boat, and it was all a dream. I had dosed off the first night on the boat, and I woke up the next day. I ran to see the captain, and He was just smiling at me. He asked if I had breakfast yet and said He would love to sit down and talk with me. The rest of the trip was all that I hoped it would be. When I got home, I was a new person. I applied to my life all the things I had learned on the island in my dream. There's not a day that goes by that I don't think about that island.

The Bible says that we are now children of God, and it tells us to consecrate ourselves, or set ourselves apart. Before the Earth was made, God set you apart for the good works. You are called to be different, not to look like the world. To be a friend of the world means you are an enemy of God. That means you may feel, at times, like you're on an island, but that doesn't mean you're alone. Jesus is always with you, and you need to know that your brothers and sisters of the faith are fighting the same battle alongside you. Now go and live out the plan God has for you, and make it a reality. Bring heaven down to Earth!

PRAYER

At your name, my enemies flee.
You opened many doors, Jesus was the key.
I was blind you helped me see.
Darkness around, you lighten my feet.
Night after night you watch over me as I sleep.
You lead, and you guide me, Lord I, your sheep.
Your angels surround me; they are your fleet.
The blood of Your Son makes my heart beat.
The cracks in my walls, were for your light to seep.
You told me to trust you, so I leapt.
I am yours, my soul you promise to keep.

BE EQUIPPED

WITH

WHAT YOU NEED TO SUCCEED

HeavenlyDose.com

Purpose Gang Publishing

x

Book Launch On Demand

Made in the USA
Middletown, DE
20 August 2022